POPULAR SONGS
HAL LEONARD
STUDENT PIANO LIBRARY

INTERMEDIATE

Piano Solos from Encanto, Frozen II, and Coco

NINE BEAUTIFUL ARRANGEMENTS BY MONA REJINO

ISBN 978-1-70516-688-8

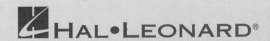

World headquarters, contact:
Hal Leonard
7777 West Bluemound Road
Milwaukee, WI 53213
Email: info@halleonard.com

In Europe, contact:
Hal Leonard Europe Limited
42 Wigmore Street
Marylebone, London, W1U 2RY
Email: info@halleonardeurope.com

In Australia, contact:
Hal Leonard Australia Pty. Ltd.
4 Lentara Court
Cheltenham, Victoria, 3192 Australia
Email: info@halleonard.com.au

Remember Me

(Lullaby)

from COCO

"For even if I'm far away, I hold you in my heart.
I sing a secret song to you each night we are apart."

Words and Music by Kristen Anderson-Lopez
and Robert Lopez
Arranged by Mona Rejino

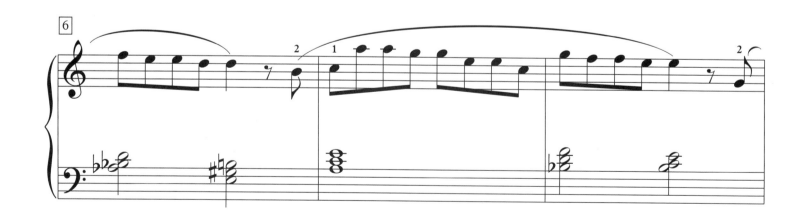

Proud Corazón
from COCO

"Our love for each other will live on forever in ev'ry beat of my proud corazón."

Music by Germaine Franco
Lyrics by Adrian Molina
Arranged by Mona Rejino

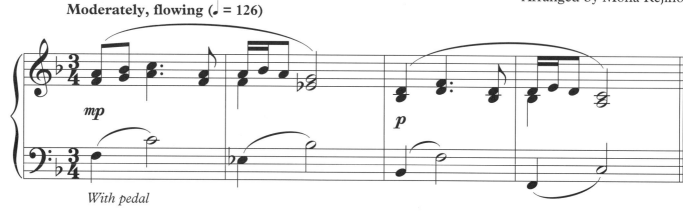

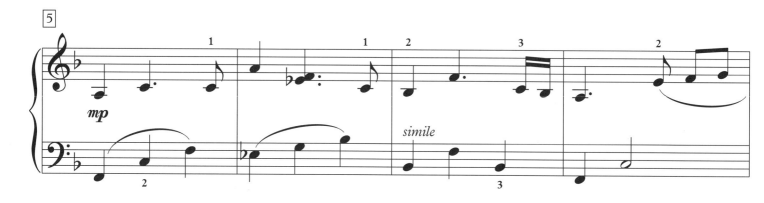

Un Poco Loco

from COCO

"I'll count it as a blessing that I'm only un poco loco."

Music by Germaine Franco
Lyrics by Adrian Molina
Arranged by Mona Rejino

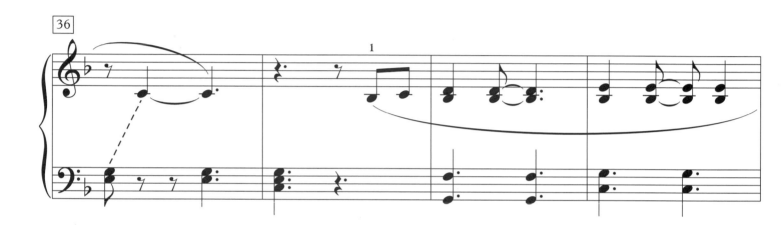

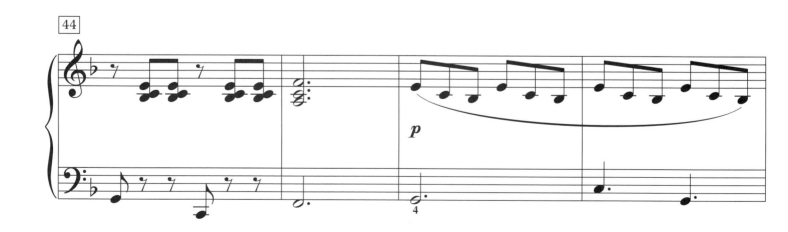

Into the Unknown
from FROZEN 2

"Don't you know there's part of me that longs to go into the unknown?"

Music and Lyrics by Kristen Anderson-Lopez
and Robert Lopez
Arranged by Mona Rejino

Mysteriosly (♩. = 104)

With pedal

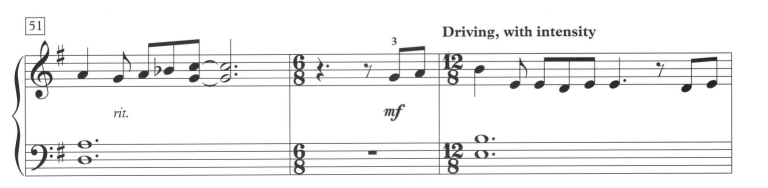

Show Yourself
from FROZEN 2

*"You're the answer I've waited for all of my life!
Oh, show yourself: let me see who you are."*

Music and Lyrics by Kristen Anderson-Lopez
and Robert Lopez
Arranged by Mona Rejino

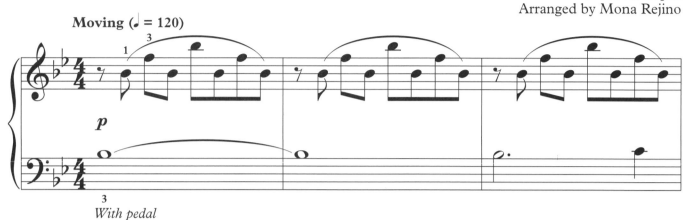

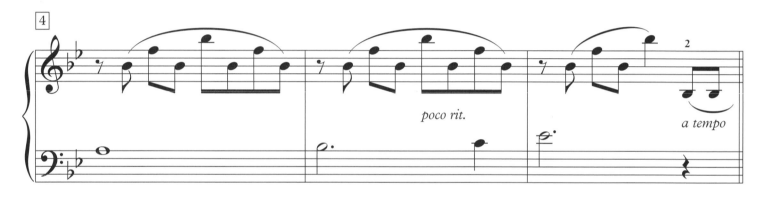

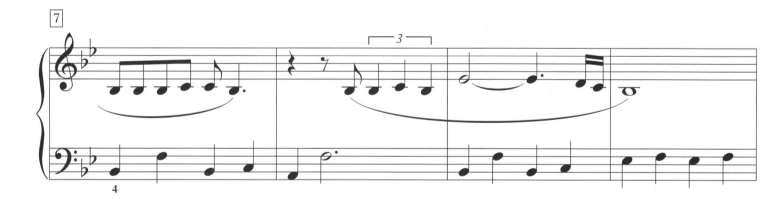

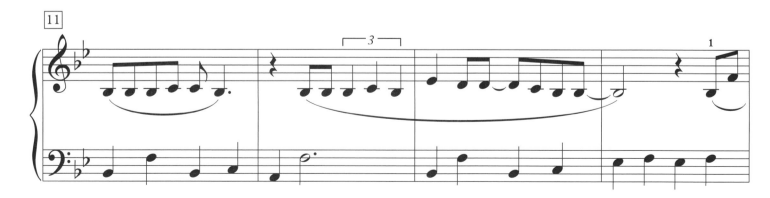

Slower, majestically

Moderately, as before

Dos Oruguitas

from ENCANTO

"Wonders await you, just on the other side.
Trust they'll be there and start to prepare the way for tomorrow."

Music and Lyrics by
Lin-Manuel Miranda
Arranged by Mona Rejino

30

Surface Pressure

from ENCANTO

"Pressure like a drip, drip, drip, that'll never stop.
Pressure that'll tip, tip, tip 'til you just go pop."

Music and Lyrics by
Lin-Manuel Miranda
Arranged by Mona Rejino

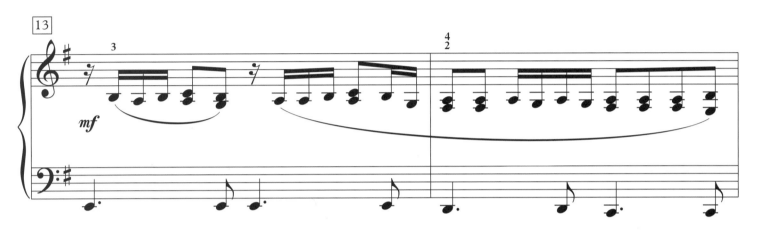

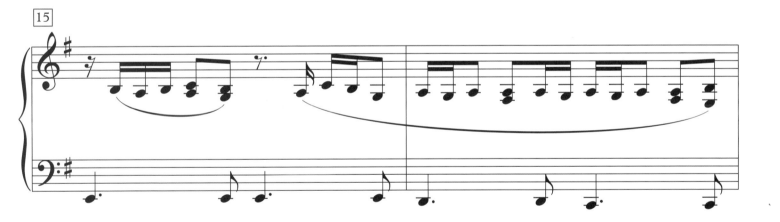

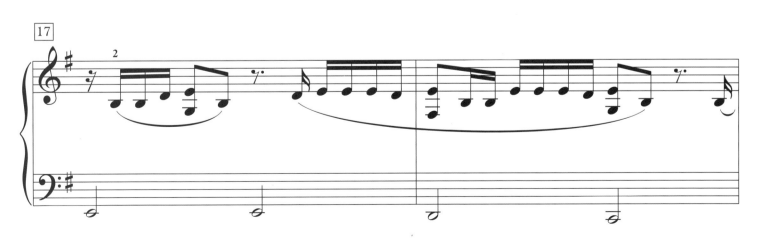

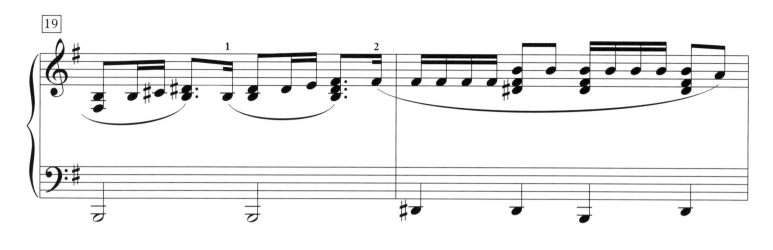

We Don't Talk About Bruno
from ENCANTO

"Not a word about Bruno!
I never should-a brought up Bruno!"

Music and Lyrics by
Lin-Manuel Miranda
Arranged by Mona Rejino

Delicately

All Is Found

from FROZEN 2

"Come, my darling, homeward bound: when all is lost, then all is found."

Music and Lyrics by Kristen Anderson-Lopez
and Robert Lopez
Arranged by Mona Rejino